AF570493

Raise Your Vibration

NIKKI SHEIKH

Raise Your Vibration

Live a Happy and Grateful Life

Copyright © 2023 Nikki Sheikh

All rights reserved

All rights reserved. This book or any portion thereof may not be reproduced, distributed or transmitted in any form or by any means without the express written consent of the copyright holder, except in the case of brief quotations for the purpose of reviews and certain other noncommercial uses permitted by copyright law.

Disclaimer:

The information contained in this book is based on research and the author's personal experiences. While the author has made every effort to ensure the accuracy and completeness of the information presented, the publisher and author assume no responsibility for errors, inaccuracies, or omissions. The reader is advised to use their judgment and discretion when implementing any information or advice provided in this book. The author and publisher are not liable for any damages or losses that may arise from the use of the information contained in this book.

The information contained in this book is not intended to substitute for professional advice or diagnosis. Readers should seek the advice of qualified professionals before implementing any of the information contained in this book.

To my dear son, loving husband, dear mother, dear father, two wonderful sisters, and one amazing brother – you are the foundation of my life and the reason why I am who I am today. Your unwavering support, encouragement, and love have been my guiding light, and I dedicate this book to each of you with gratitude and appreciation. To my son, may you always follow your dreams with determination and purpose. To my husband, may our love continue to thrive and grow. To my mother, may your wise counsel and guidance continue to inspire me. To my father, may your strength and courage always guide me. To my sisters and brother, may our bond continue to be a source of comfort and joy. Thank you for being the shining stars in my life.

Dear Reader,

I am so grateful that you have chosen to pick up this book on raising your vibration. I believe that everything in life is energy and that raising our vibration can attract more positivity, abundance, and joy into our lives.

This book is about taking action, cultivating self-awareness, and making conscious choices that align with our highest selves. In the pages that follow, you will find practical exercises, insights, and tools to help you increase your energetic frequency. Remember, you have the power to create the life you want, and by raising your vibration, you can manifest your deepest desires.

I encourage you to approach this book with an open mind and heart and to take the time to reflect on how the teachings and practices can be applied to your own life. If you find yourself resonating with the message, please share it with others who may benefit from this work.

With love and gratitude,

Nikki Sheikh

Contents

Preface

"Raise Your Vibration: Live A Happy and Grateful Life" by Nikki Sheikh is a comprehensive guide to understanding and utilizing the power of vibrational energy to improve your well-being. The author of this book discusses the idea of vibrational energy and how it affects both our physical and mental health. The book is broken down into fourteen chapters, each of which focuses on a certain strategy that can assist readers in raising their vibration and generally improving the quality of their lives.

The book includes numerous daily rituals that readers may easily incorporate into their lives, such as thankfulness, affirmations of gratitude, and meditation. These exercises are intended to assist readers in letting go of negative energy, connecting with their inner selves, and increasing their vibratory frequency. Anyone looking to enhance their mental and emotional well-being, and find more happiness and contentment in life will find something to their liking in this book.

Chapter1: - Understanding Vibrational Energy

Thank you for visiting this book on boosting your vibration. We will discuss vibrational energy in this chapter, including what it is, why it's significant, and how it impacts your life.

The frequency of energy that you emit through your thoughts, feelings, and deeds is referred to as vibrational energy. Depending on your mental state and the energy you are radiating out into the world, this energy can be high or low. Raising your vibrations entails raising your energy's frequency, which can improve your mood, level of energy, and general well-being. We'll look at various techniques in this book that will help you uplift your vibration and have a more fulfilling existence.

WHAT IS VIBRATIONAL ENERGY: -

All things and creatures, including people, give off energy that vibrates at a particular frequency. Increasing your vibrations entails raising your energy's frequency. This can be accomplished in several ways, such as through meditation, optimistic thinking, and surrounding oneself with positive people. Raising your vibrations causes you to release positive energy, which draws great situations into your life.

Raising your vibration is crucial because low-frequency energy can draw in bad experiences like financial hardship, tense relationships, and unfulfilling work. High-frequency energy, on the other hand, might draw favorable events like good health, satisfying relationships, and professional achievement. You can strengthen your spiritual awareness, attract abundance and success, and take better care of your physical and mental health by boosting your vibration.

We will look at various techniques in this book that can help you uplift your vibration and lead a more fulfilling life. We'll look into several methods, including affirmations of appreciation, meditation, and self-care. You can raise the frequency of your energy and bring good things into your life by implementing these techniques into your everyday routine. Living a happy and prosperous life requires understanding and boosting your vibrations. You can enhance your general well-being and attract positive experiences by emanating positive energy.

DEFINING VIBRATIONAL ENERGY.

Consider yourself a radio station sending a signal out into the universe. Your energy, which is composed of your ideas, feelings, and deeds, is the source of this signal. When you're joyful and upbeat, you're sending out a high-frequency signal that, like a magnet, pulls happy experiences back to you. Any number of excellent things can happen, such as making new friends, getting a new job, or just feeling good about yourself.

On the other side, when you're feeling bad, upset, or depressed, you're sending out a low-frequency signal that draws bad things to you. You can discover that life isn't as enjoyable as you'd like it to be because you keep hitting roadblocks, people appear unfriendly to you, or all three. By matching your energy's frequency to the frequency of the events you draw, the Law of Attraction works. Consequently, it's critical to put your attention on feeling good, having positive ideas, and acting positively if you want to attract more positive experiences into your life.

Naturally, it's not always simple to be upbeat and joyful all the time. But the more you work on being grateful for and concentrating on the wonderful things in your life, the nicer things will start to happen to you. You have to tune your energy to the proper frequency to attract the experiences you want. It's like setting your radio station to the right frequency so you can hear your favorite music.

LOW VIBRATIONS

One sign of being in a low-frequency state of consciousness is having restricted perception or having trouble understanding particular events or experiences. Numerous things, like a lack of mindfulness or self-awareness, unfavorable thought patterns, or an inflated ego that blocks the flow of life force, might contribute to this.

We are less able to communicate with our inner selves and the world around us when we are in a low-frequency state of consciousness. Negative emotions and limiting beliefs may skew our perceptions and interpretations of events, making it challenging to grasp the large picture or comprehend the full ramifications of our choices.

Increasing our awareness of our thoughts and emotions is one method to leave a low-frequency condition. We may learn a lot about our vibratory frequency and the energy we are sending out into the world by observing our emotions. By focusing on our emotions, we can begin to spot trends and triggers that might be causing our low-frequency state. A potent technique to enhance our vibration and enter a higher frequency level of consciousness is to choose thoughts that make us feel emotionally pleasant. This entails deliberately choosing to dwell on uplifting, upbeat ideas and experiences rather than on stressful or bad circumstances..

Chapter 2: - Practicing Gratitude

Gratitude practice is one of the most effective strategies to boost your vibration. Being grateful is giving thanks for your blessings rather than dwelling on your shortcomings. When you concentrate on your blessings, your energy is directed toward abundance and optimism. You may be able to draw more of the same into your life by doing this.

This chapter will discuss various techniques for cultivating thankfulness, including maintaining a gratitude notebook, thanking others, and looking for the positive side of difficult circumstances.

WHAT IS THANKFULNESS, AND WHY SHOULD WE VALUE IT?

Practicing thankfulness is a terrific place to start if you're searching for a quick and efficient strategy to improve your mental and physical health. Taking the time to recognize and be grateful for the positive aspects of our lives has several advantages that can make us feel happier, healthier, and more content.

The ability to concentrate on the positive aspects of our lives rather than dwelling on the negative is one of the key advantages of practicing thankfulness. This can have a significant impact on our outlook on life and mood, lowering tension, anxiety, and depressive symptoms. Studies have shown that those who routinely express appreciation tend to be happier and more positive.

People who practice thankfulness have been shown to have higher sleep quality and a stronger immune system, which can help to prevent disease and improve general health, according to studies. Gratitude exercises can help strengthen our interpersonal connections. By expressing our thanks to others, we fortify our bonds and create deeper, more satisfying ties. Better communication, more empathy, and a stronger sense of connection to those around us may result from this.

There are numerous easy strategies to cultivate gratitude, including journaling about our blessings, saying "thank you" more frequently, or just setting aside some time each day to think about all the good things in our life. Whatever approach you use, including thankfulness in your daily life can have a significant and beneficial impact on your well-being.

HOW TO PRACTICE GRATITUDE DAILY?

following are some varied strategies to include appreciation in your daily routine:

KEEP A NOTEBOOK OF GRATITUDE:

Every day, list three things for which you are grateful. This fosters an appreciation for your life and helps you pay attention to its positive parts.

MEDITATE:

Spend a few minutes every day in meditation, concentrating on the things in your life for which you are grateful. By doing so, you may be able to change your perspective to one of thankfulness and increase the abundance in your life.

BE THANKFUL FOR OTHERS:

Express your thanks to others by taking the time to let them know how much you value them. This might be as easy as texting someone or writing them a thank-you note.

AFFIRMATIONS:

Use affirmations to your advantage. Include expressions of appreciation in your daily affirmations. Use phrases like "I'm grateful for the abundance in my life" or "I attract good things through my gratitude. "

TAKE A WALK OF GRATITUDE:

take the time to appreciate the beauty of the natural world around you. For a relaxing walk, pick a peaceful natural area like a park, beach, or hiking trail. Take a moment to center yourself and pay attention to your surroundings before starting your walk.

Set a goal for your walk, such as appreciating nature's beauty or improving your physical and mental health. Keep in mind and give thanks for the things in your environment as you walk, such as the breathtaking view or the feel of the ground beneath your feet.

Recognize the colors, textures, scents, tastes, and sensations in your environment to increase your appreciation of it. Say encouraging things to yourself aloud while being grateful for the abundance in your life or the love and support of your family and friends.

Spend some time reflecting on your blessings and expressing your thanks for them. End your walk by thanking God for allowing you to walk and enjoy the beauty of the earth. Make a mental note to keep practicing gratitude in your everyday life.

You may attract more riches into your life and develop a more optimistic outlook by incorporating thankfulness into your everyday practice.

Chapter 3: - Practice Meditation

Meditation is another powerful method for raising vibration. You can feel more centered and at peace when you meditate because it helps you quiet your thoughts and connect with your inner self. There are numerous varieties of meditation, including mindfulness meditation, meditation on loving-kindness, and visualization meditation. We'll discuss these many kinds in this chapter and offer advice on how to begin meditating.

DIFFERENT TYPES OF MEDITATION TECHNIQUES.

There are numerous meditation methods with various purposes and advantages. Meditation emphasizes present-moment awareness and objectively observing one's thoughts and feelings. Several well-liked methods of meditation include.

1) **TRANSCENDENTAL MEDITATION** uses mantras or other repetitive sounds to quiet the mind and induce deep relaxation.
2) Compassion and kindness towards oneself and others are developed through **LOVING-KINDNESS MEDITATION.**
3) **BODY SCAN MEDITATION**, which releases tension and encourages relaxation, includes paying methodical attention to various parts of the body.
4) Using a meditation recording to guide you through the practice with a particular aim or focus is known as **GUIDED MEDITATION.**
5) **YOGA MEDITATION** is a practice that blends breathing exercises, bodily postures, and meditation to enhance both mental and physical well-being.
6) **CHAKRA MEDITATION** promotes harmony and balance between the mind, body, and spirit by focusing on the seven energy centers in the body.
7) **MINDFULNESS MEDITATION:** - Being present in the here and now, free from distraction and judgment, is the foundation of mindfulness meditation. With a curious and accepting mindset, this type of meditation tries to develop awareness and observation of one's thoughts, emotions, and physical sensations.

HERE'S A GUIDE TO PRACTICING MINDFULNESS MEDITATION:

1) Find an area that is peaceful and comfortable where you may sit alone first. You can decide whether it feels more comfortable to sit on a cushion on the floor or a chair.
2) Close your eyes or avert your look while maintaining a straight back. Put your hands down on your lap, palms either up or down.
3) Breathe in deeply through your nose and out through your mouth for a few breaths. Permit your body to unwind as you breathe out.
4) Pay close attention to the sensation of your breath as it enters and exits your body. You can focus on how your chest and abdomen move or the air that is entering your nose.
5) You could notice that your thoughts begin to stray while you focus on your breathing. This is expected

and normal. Simply identify the thought or emotion when you catch yourself daydreaming, then gently bring your attention back to your breathing.

6) Stay away from analyzing or criticizing your thoughts. Instead, just watch them as they pass by. Keep in mind that the goal is to just watch your thoughts without being sucked into them.

7) Spend some time focusing just on your breath while allowing yourself to fully inhabit the present moment.

8) Take a few deep breaths when you're ready to end the meditation, and then slowly open your eyes. Observe your feelings for a time, then return your focus to the present. You'll find that with regular practice, you are more adept at maintaining present-moment awareness and handling difficult situations.

HOW TO INCLUDE MEDITATION IN YOUR REGULAR ACTIVITIES?

There are some practical suggestions to get you started on incorporating meditation into your everyday routine.

- Pick a time of day that suits you best to start, such as just before bed or in the morning. As you become more accustomed to the practice, progressively extend your meditation sessions from the initial few minutes.

- Locate a distraction-free area that is quiet, such as a meditation room or a private area of your home.
- Use a guided meditation app or recording if you struggle to meditate alone.
- Make it a habit to meditate at the same time each day since consistency is important.

Keep in mind that it takes time and practice to experience the advantages of meditation. You can establish a regular meditation practice that aids in stress relief and general well-being with time and practice

Chapter 4: - Inspire yourself

By surrounding yourself with inspiration sources that speak to you, you can create inspiration in your life. This can include things like other people, literature, music, and artwork that enliven and motivate you.

LISTEN TO A MOTIVATIONAL SPEAKER

Start by thinking about the individuals in your life. Find people who inspire you, whether they be close friends, relatives, co-workers, or mentors. Spend time with them and pay attention to the routines and actions that inspire you. Talk to them and enquire about their opinions and ideas. You can improve your thinking and increase your motivation to accomplish your goals by surrounding yourself with positive and motivated people.

READ BOOKS

Look for books that speak to you and motivate you to action. Self-help books, biographies of accomplished people, and other works of literature that speak to you can fall under this category. You can also research various musical genres that inspire you and make playlists to listen to all day.

You should acquaint yourself with inspiring art. This can include any work of art that speaks to you, whether it be a painting, a sculpture, a photograph, or another medium. Visit exhibitions, museums, or art galleries that include inspiring or motivating pieces of art.

You may consciously build a more upbeat and motivated mindset, which can assist you in reaching your objectives and leading a satisfying life, by actively seeking out and surrounding yourself with sources of inspiration.

WATCH INSPIRATIONAL MOVIE

Watching motivational movies can be a great method to increase motivation, discover fresh viewpoints, and spark creativity. Movies can arouse emotions and light a fire within us, whether it's a biopic about a great entrepreneur or a sports film that demonstrates the strength of determination.

you deserve a life
full of happiness
and positivity

Chapter 5: - Exercise

Exercise is beneficial for your physical health as well as for raising vibration. Your body releases endorphins when you exercise, which can help improve your mood and energy levels.

This chapter will examine many forms of exercise, including yoga, dancing, and cardio, that can help you boost your vibration. We'll also offer advice on how to include fitness in your daily routine.

HOW EXERCISING AFFECTS YOUR VIBRATIONS

Our emotional health, including our mood and stress levels, can benefit from exercise. Exercise has been demonstrated to release endorphins, which are organic compounds that can help elevate mood and lessen symptoms of worry and despair. This is one of the main reasons for this. By acting as natural painkillers and assisting in the reduction of stress and anxiety, these endorphins make us feel less tense and more upbeat.

Exercise can boost our physical energy and vitality in addition to releasing endorphins. Regular exercise has been demonstrated to improve muscular strength, cardiovascular fitness, and endurance, all of which contribute to a general sense of well-being and optimism.

After a workout, when we may feel more alert, focused, and enthusiastic, this increase in physical energy may be more obvious. Exercise can also help us sleep better, which can lead to feeling more physical and emotional well-being.

Physical activity can also give us a sense of accomplishment and raise our self-esteem. Setting and achieving fitness objectives can give us a sense of accomplishment and self-assurance, which can enhance our general outlook on life and well-being. In addition to helping us connect with people who share our interests and ambitions, exercise can also serve as a social outlet, which can boost our spirits and sense of belonging.

Exercise and boosting vibrations, or positive energy, are linked in a variety of ways. Exercise can promote general well-being and positivity by releasing endorphins, boosting physical energy, enhancing sleep quality, and creating a sense of accomplishment and community.

HOW TO INCLUDE EXERCISE IN YOUR EVERYDAY ROUTINE?

One of the finest methods to enhance your general health and well-being is by including exercise in your daily routine. You can use this straightforward advice to accomplish this:

- Make an achievable workout goal for yourself. Start your daily workout routine, for instance, with 30 minutes and progressively increase it.
- Make a program for your daily workout regimen, being sure to pick an hour that suits you the most. This will aid in developing a habit of exercising.
- If you've never exercised before, start with easy workouts like stretching, walking, or running. As you advance, gradually increase the duration and intensity of your workouts.
- It takes consistency to get results. Make an effort to follow your routine as closely as you can and work out at least three to four times every week.
- Utilize technology to monitor your development and maintain motivation. You can accomplish your goals with the help of one of the various fitness apps or trackers that are available.

- Pick activities you enjoy, such as swimming, hiking, or dancing. This will help you stick to your plan and make exercise enjoyable.

Do not forget that adding exercise to your routine does not need to be difficult or time-consuming. You may attain your fitness goals and enhance your general health by starting small, being consistent, and having fun.

Chapter 6: - Aromatherapy

Using essential oils that have been derived from various plant parts, aromatherapy encourages mental, emotional, and spiritual well-being. For generations, it has been used to improve mood, reduce tension, and promote relaxation. By fostering a sense of harmony, balance, and clarity, essential oils can also assist elevate a person's vibration, which is a term used to describe their energy level.

One's vibration can be raised by using a variety of essential oils, each of which has special qualities that have a particular impact on the body and mind.

- For instance, lavender oil is well-known for its calming and relaxing qualities that can help people feel less stressed and anxious while also enhancing their sense of peace and well-being.

- Another illustration is lemon oil, which has energizing and uplifting qualities that improve mood, focus, and concentration.
- Grounding properties of frankincense oil help to foster sensations of tranquility and tranquility. It benefits from improving meditation and spiritual practices.
- Refreshing and energizing peppermint oil helps increase energy and enhance mental clarity.

You can put a few drops of your preferred essential oil into a diffuser or oil burner and breathe in the aroma to employ aromatherapy to raise your vibration. Adding a few drops to a bath or applying the combination to your skin after combining essential oils with carrier oils like jojoba or almond oil.

start an alternative healing
from natural resources

It is very important to keep in mind that essential oils are quite potent and should be used with caution. Always dilute essential oils before applying them to the skin, and keep them away from delicate regions like the eyes and mouth. It is best to speak with a healthcare provider before using essential oils if you have any health issues, is pregnant, or are nursing.

Chapter 7: - Connect with Nature

We can raise our vibrations by connecting with nature, which has a way of anchoring and centering us. You can feel more at ease and tranquil when you spend time in nature, whether you go on a walk or just sit in a park.

This chapter will discuss the advantages of being in touch with nature and offer advice on how to do so, even if you live in a city.

THE HEALING POWER OF NATURE.

There is increasing evidence to support the notion that nature has healing properties. Our physical, mental, and emotional health can benefit greatly from time spent in nature.

The immune system can be strengthened and overall health can be improved through exposure to natural factors like sunlight, clean air, and soil microbes. This improves physical health.

The hormone cortisol, which is linked to stress, is demonstrated to be decreased when people are in nature, while endorphin production is increased, which can boost mood and lessen anxiety. The calming influence of nature on the mind helps lessen the symptoms of mental health issues including sadness and anxiety.

Time spent outdoors has been related to enhancements in cognitive abilities like better focus, memory, and creativity. The ability of nature to provide a holistic approach to health and well-being, addressing not just physical ailments but also mental and emotional health, is the source of its healing power.

Making a connection with nature can help people heal and grow as well as provide them with a sense of tranquillity and calm.

DIFFERENT WAYS TO CONNECT WITH NATURE.

There are many methods to connect with nature, some of which include:

HIKING AND WALKING:

These activities are great for getting outside and discovering nature. This activity allows you to breathe in some fresh air, enjoy the beauty of nature, and exercise.

GARDENING: -

Gardening gives you a hands-on chance to interact with natural elements like plants and soil. It can be a great way to feel a connection to the natural world.

CAMPING: -

A terrific method to become fully immersed in nature is to spend the night outside. It provides a chance to switch off from technology and take in the natural environment.

MEDITATING OUTSIDE: -

Spending time in nature and finding inner serenity are two benefits of outdoor meditation. It enables one to focus on the present, unwind mentally, and savor the beauty of nature.

SWIMMING: -

Swimming in rivers or lakes, or other natural bodies of water, can be a terrific way to be in touch with nature. It provides a chance to take in the natural beauty of the surroundings while exercising.

OBSERVING ANIMALS: -

Getting closer to nature can be enjoyable when you observe wildlife in its natural setting. It allows admiring the diversity and beauty of the natural world while learning about the environment.

Picnicking: -

Having a picnic with loved ones outside is a simple way to be close to nature. It enables people to take in the beauty of nature while spending time with others.

Overall, there are many methods to interact with nature; people should select the ones that make them feel the happiest and most relaxed.

How Being in Nature Might Make You Vibrate Higher

Your energetic state and vibration can be affected by nature in a variety of ways. First of all, being in a natural setting like a forest, a mountain, or an ocean can lower stress levels and promote peace and relaxation, which raises vibrational frequencies.

Second, grounding your energy and releasing bad energy by walking barefoot on the ground, a practice known as "earthing," can raise your vibratory frequency in general. Exposure to sunlight and fresh air can raise your vibratory state because sunlight creates serotonin, which is associated with happiness and well-being.

Last but not least, everything in nature vibrates at a specific, individual frequency. By connecting with these frequencies, you can harmonize your vibration with nature's vibration, which encourages tranquillity and relaxation. All things considered, spending time outdoors and making connections with the natural world can significantly raise your vibratory state, fostering harmony, stillness, and energy.

WALKING BAREFOOT IN NATURE

The process of "earthing" or "grounding" involves walking barefoot on natural surfaces like grass, sand, or soil. Your body will be electrically connected to the Earth through this practice. Negative electrons are abundant on Earth; they can have a balancing effect on a person's body.

The idea behind earthing is that we can eliminate any bad energy or blockages that may be held in our bodies by connecting to the energy of the Earth. Because of this, good, higher-frequency energies can pass through us. In addition to raising our vibration, grounding can promote emotions of serenity, equilibrium, and a sense of connection to nature. Being barefoot on grassy or other natural surfaces is an efficient approach to boosting your vibration, connecting with nature, and supporting your physical and emotional well-being.

Chapter 8: - Random Gestures of Generosity

Random acts of kindness can make you and others around you feel better since they show others that you have compassion and generosity. You may improve your level of positive energy by making these gestures, which may then help you attract more positivity into your life. To increase your frequency, consider the following instances of random acts of kindness:

COMPLIMENT SOMEONE: Give a sincere compliment to someone you come across throughout the day. This might relate to how they seem, what they do, or a quality they possess that is admirable.

PAY IT FORWARD by treating the person in line behind you to lunch or coffee. As the recipient may be motivated to spread compassion on their own, this can have a domino effect.

OFFER TO ASSIST SOMEONE who is having trouble with a task, such as lifting large luggage or finishing a labor project. Someone who is in need can benefit from your willingness to assist them.

MAKE TIME TO ACTIVELY LISTEN TO SOMEONE who needs to speak by paying close attention to them. Demonstrate your empathy and support without passing judgment or interfering.

SEND NICE NOTES TO FRIENDS, FAMILY MEMBERS, or anyone else you haven't spoken to in a while. Let them know they are on your mind and that you value them.

CHARITY: Volunteer your time by helping a neighborhood charity or civic group. This may be a fantastic way to engage with others and give back to your community.

Simply smiling and being amiable to others around you can foster a nice environment and make someone's day.

Always keep in mind that these deeds of compassion don't have to be complicated or impressive. Even the smallest acts of kindness can have a big influence on people's lives and your own. You can improve your pleasure and feeling of purpose while also making a difference in the world by purposefully trying to carry out these deeds of kindness.

Chapter 9: - Healthy Ways to Release Negative Emotions

Finding healthy ways to release negative emotions is very important to live a happy and healthy life, below are a few of them

EXERCISE REGULARLY: -

Regular exercise can help to enhance mood, boost energy levels, and reduce stress and worry. Running, yoga, and weightlifting are examples of effective exercises.

MAINTAIN A JOURNAL: -

Writing in a journal is a writing technique that enables you to put your ideas and emotions on paper. It is a therapeutic method that can assist you in processing and coping with unpleasant feelings. You must locate a secluded, calm area where you may write without being disturbed or distracted if you want to use journaling as a release mechanism for unpleasant feelings.

To give yourself a dedicated time to write, set a timer for 10-15 minutes once you have located a suitable area. Write about the unfavorable feelings you are experiencing at this time. It's crucial to write freely without worrying about your grammar, spelling, or punctuation. Without any restraint, let your thoughts and emotions flow onto the paper.

Investigate the sources of your bad feelings as you write. Find out what caused this emotion by asking yourself "What triggered this emotion?" or "What beliefs or assumptions am I holding that are contributing to this feeling?" You can better understand your emotions and start to let them go by looking into the sources.

Write as much as you need to accurately convey your feelings and thoughts. Do not limit yourself or hold back. The idea is to get those unpleasant feelings out of your body and head.

Take a few deep breaths once you've completed writing so that you may truly feel and experience the discharge of your unpleasant feelings. Although going through this can be emotionally taxing, it's crucial to give yourself time to digest your feelings.

You can also decide to cut up or burn the pages you wrote on as a symbolic gesture of letting go of your unfavorable emotions if you feel comfortable doing so. This may be a potent method for expelling negative energy and moving on with more clarity and calm.

This method of journaling can help you better understand your unpleasant feelings, let them go of your body and mind, and move on with more clarity and calm. It can be a useful method for controlling and overcoming challenging emotions.

PRACTICE MINDFULNESS MEDITATION: -

This method entails concentrating on the right now without passing judgment. The benefits of mindfulness meditation include improved mood, relaxation, and a decrease in stress and anxiety. I went into great length about it in chapter 3.

CREATIVE EXPRESSION: -

can be a good method to let go of bad emotions. For example, painting, drawing, or music-making are all examples of creative activities. You can feel accomplished and express yourself through these activities.

SPEAK TO SOMEONE: -

At times, expressing unpleasant feelings to a dependable friend or therapist might be beneficial. They can offer assistance, direction, and a sympathetic ear.

Everybody is unique, therefore it's vital to keep in mind that what works for one person might not work for another. Therefore, it's crucial to discover appropriate coping mechanisms that suit you for letting go of your unpleasant feelings.

Chapter 10: - Listen to Music

Our emotions are strongly influenced by music, and it can also boost our energy. Our attitude and level of energy might be affected differently by various forms of music.

We'll look at how music influences our vibrations in this chapter and offer some advice on how to use music to feel better and have more energy. We'll also play you a few of our favorite upbeat tracks!

THE IMPACT OF MUSIC ON YOUR VIBRATIONS

The vibrations or general energy level of a person can be significantly influenced by music. This is because music activates many brain regions, leading to emotional reactions as well as physical responses in the body.

The heart rate, breathing rate, and general level of energy can all be affected by the rhythm and melody of music. For instance, music that is energetic and fast-paced might make someone feel more energized, while soothing music that is slow-paced and relaxing can help people unwind and feel less stressed.

The lyrics of a song, in addition to its rhythm and melody, can influence a listener's vibrations. While negative or depressing lyrics can elicit feelings of melancholy and anxiety, positive and uplifting songs can inspire sentiments of joy and happiness. music can affect a person's mood and level of energy. It's critical to select music that reflects your intended vibrations and aids in achieving the right emotional state.

There are several advantages to listening to music for the body and mind. Several benefits are as follows:

REDUCES ANXIETY AND STRESS: -

Listening to peaceful music can help lower anxiety and stress levels. Additionally, it may offer physical advantages including decreasing blood pressure and enhancing well-being.

ENHANCES MOOD: -

Music has the power to affect our emotions, and listening to music can uplift our spirits and promote relaxation and motivation.

ENHANCES COGNITIVE FUNCTION: -

Listening to music can enhance cognition by sharpening focus, memory, and attention.

DIFFERENT KINDS OF MUSIC CAN UPLIFT YOUR SPIRIT

Different kinds of music can uplift your energy and foster a sense of well-being. Here are a few illustrations:

CLASSICAL MUSIC: -

The calming and soothing effects of classical music on the body and mind are well-known. It can lower tension and anxiety levels while encouraging relaxation.

UPBEAT MUSIC: -

Upbeat music with a quick tempo will speed up breathing and the heart rate, which can raise energy and elevate mood.

NATURE'S NOISES can help to soothe the mind and body, including the sounds of rain, waves, and bird song. It can encourage relaxation and lower stress levels.

CHANTS AND MANTRAS: -

Chants and mantras are frequently used in meditation techniques and can help people feel at ease and peaceful. They can aid in mental peace and stress reduction.

INSTRUMENTAL MUSIC: -

Calming and relaxing instrumental music includes piano, guitar, and violin. It can aid in lowering stress levels and fostering a feeling of well-being.

It's crucial to remember that everyone may have different musical tastes and responses. One person's solution might not be suitable for another. Therefore, it's crucial to listen to music that matches your interests and makes you feel joyful and content.

Chapter 11: - Laughter

The finest medicine is laughter, which also helps increase our vibrations. Endorphins, which are released when we laugh and can assist improve our mood and energy levels.

We'll discuss the advantages of laughter in this chapter and provide you with some suggestions on how to add more laughter to your life, like watching a humorous movie or hanging out with people who make you laugh.

HOW LAUGHTER RAISES OUR VIBRATION

When we laugh, our bodies respond physically and chemically, which benefits our health and wellness. Endorphins are released when we laugh, which can make us feel good and help us feel less stressed and anxious. Additionally, laughter causes vibrations in the body that can enhance both our physical and mental health. Our bodies vibrate at various frequencies, and laughter can increase our frequency to support health and well-being, according to the tenets of vibrational medicine.

Laughter can improve our energy and mood in a variety of ways. Laughing can lower blood pressure, strengthen our immune system, and reduce stress and anxiety. Additionally, it can change our energies and produce a happy, peaceful mood that enhances our sense of general welfare and connectedness to the outside world.

There are various methods to make our life more humorous.

- We can practice laughter yoga
- play activities that involve laughter
- watch comedic movies or TV shows
- read funny books or comic strips
- spend time with friends who make us laugh
- attempt laughter therapy to encourage healing and well-being.

Including laughter in our regular activities can significantly improve our mood and sense of wellness. So go ahead and laugh out loud; it will do you good!

MULTIPLE WAYS OF INCLUDING LAUGHTER IN YOUR LIFE

You may increase your daily laughter in m any ways. One easy method is to watch or listen to something hilarious, such as a sitcom, stand-up comedy program, or funny podcast. It's a simple way to add some humor to your day. It might be an excellent way to lift your spirits and make you chuckle to **watch comedies and light movies**. When you see something hilarious or light-hearted, it can help you relax and enjoy the moment by taking your mind off of any concerns or problems you might be having.

Spending time with others who make you laugh and have a fantastic sense of humor is another approach to include laughing. Being around people who make you laugh and smile can help lift your spirits and make you feel better since laughter is contagious.

It's also crucial to develop a sense of humor and to stop taking yourself too seriously. Be confident in your ability to laugh at your flaws and inadequacies. Having a good laugh at yourself might help you feel better about yourself and lessen stress.

Playing games, completing puzzles, or engaging in any other entertaining activity might be a terrific way to increase your capacity for laughter. It aids in your ability to relax and have fun, which is crucial to leading a happy existence.

A different technique to incorporate laughter into your life is **laughter yoga**, which combines deep breathing with laughter exercises. It's a fantastic approach to increase laughter and enjoy the associated health advantages. It might also assist to increase your everyday laughs by telling jokes or amusing stories to pals. It's a great method to raise the energy level and foster a happier atmosphere.

Last but not least, finding humor in everyday occurrences can make it easier for you to see the bright side of things and bring more laughter and joy into your life. You might come across an amusing occurrence, a clever insight, or a witty remark. The most happiness and laughter can come from these little things in life.

Chapter 12: - Self-Care

It's easy to overlook self-care with everything going on in our hectic lives. But it's crucial to keep in mind that self-care is essential for preserving both our physical and mental well-being.

We may lower our stress levels, increase our energy levels, and enhance our general well-being by making time for ourselves. To live a happy and healthy life, don't forget to prioritize taking care of yourself!

It involves making time for yourself and engaging in leisure activities that promote peace and personal growth. Common self-care methods include:

- Exercise
- healthy eating
- Getting adequate sleep Spending time in

  nature

- Using mindfulness or meditation
- Taking a bath and reading a book
- spending time with family and friends
- pursuing a hobby

WHY IT'S IMPORTANT TO TAKE CARE OF ONESELF

For several reasons, it's crucial to look for yourself:

REDUCED STRESS AND ANXIETY: -

Self-care activities can assist you in lowering your stress and anxiety levels. It can aid in your relaxation and recharge, making it simpler for you to deal with the difficulties of life.

PHYSICALLY BETTER: -

Exercise and a healthy diet are two self-care practices that can help you achieve better physical health. You may maintain a healthy weight, lower your chance of developing chronic diseases, and increase your general fitness by engaging in regular exercise.

MENTAL HEALTH: -

Self-care is an effective way to maintain or regain your mental health. You can boost your mood and manage your stress and anxiety by engaging in practices like meditation and mindfulness.

Taking care of yourself helps you focus and be more effective. You can use this to succeed in both your personal and professional life and reach your goals.

SELF-CARE IS SELF-LOVE: -

A key aspect of self-love is self-care. Taking care of your physical, emotional, and mental needs demonstrates your appreciation for and worth of yourself. It entails setting aside time for activities that make you happy, calm, and focused. Exercise, meditation, quality time with close friends and family, and indulgence in passion are just a few examples of self-care practices.

Making self-care a priority is a way to communicate to yourself that you deserve to be happy and healthy and that your well-being is significant. You can become more robust, self-assured, and equipped to deal with life's obstacles as a result of practicing self-love and self-care.

TIPS ON HOW YOU CAN LOOK AFTER YOURSELF:

It's simple to engage in self-care. Here are a few quick methods to get going:

INVEST IN YOURSELF:-

Your calendar should include time for self-care activities. Don't allow anything else to interfere with this visit; treat it just like any other.

START SMALL: -

To engage in self-care, you don't have to make significant lifestyle adjustments. Start with little adjustments like scheduling time to read a book before going to bed or going for a walk during your lunch break.

KEEP IT CONSISTENT: -

Make taking care of yourself a regular part of your day. The secret to self-care is consistency.

BE KIND TO YOURSELF: -

Remind yourself to be gentle with yourself. Don't be hard on yourself if you forget to practice self-care. Simply resume where you left off and proceed.

Chapter 13: - Learn to Forgive

It's important to understand that harboring resentment towards someone for a protracted period might start to negatively impact your physical health. It is not worthwhile to carry such weight around. By harboring anger against the person who injured you, you are essentially hurting yourself rather than the offender. Therefore, it's critical to develop our capacity for forgiving those who have wronged us in the past.

Forgiving someone doesn't imply that you forget what happened or approve of what they did to do you harm. It involves letting go of the unfavorable feelings and animosity you've been holding onto. You must choose forgiveness for yourself, not for the other person.

By forgiving someone, you release yourself from the weight of resentment and animosity. You're permitting yourself to let go of the past and put your attention on the present and the future.

It may take some time and effort to completely let go of unpleasant emotions because forgiveness is a process. But it's worthwhile for your own mental and physical health.

It's important to keep in mind that forgiving someone is about you, not about them. You're simply harming yourself if you keep your bitterness and rage inside. You're making yourself suffer because of something someone else did. You may regulate your emotions and free yourself from the burden of regrettable previous experiences by forgiving someone.

Therefore, practice forgiving those who have wronged you in the past. It's a potent means of bringing healing and calms into your life. Be patient with yourself and take your time, but keep in mind that the journey is worthwhile. Keep in mind that forgiveness is about you and your well-being, not about the other person.

Chapter 14: - Heal Your Inner Child

Healing your inner child might be a good first step towards feeling better if you have bad childhood experiences that are harming you. If ignored, your inner child—which is the part of you that has your earliest experiences, feelings, and beliefs—can have a big impact on your life.

It's critical to accept your inner child's existence and realize that it requires your care and attention if you want to begin healing it. Making a secure and comfortable space through visualization, meditation, or writing is one approach to getting in touch with your inner child.

FIND YOUR TRIGGERS

Finding your triggers is essential to resolving your inner child issues. Negative events or circumstances known as triggers can set off emotional reactions that have an impact on your relationships, habits, and emotions. By becoming aware of your triggers, you can address the trauma's underlying causes and create coping mechanisms.

SIT WITH YOUR EMOTIONS

Self-compassion training is a crucial component of resolving your inner child issues. Accepting your emotions and feelings without condemnation or self-blame can be facilitated by treating oneself with respect, care, and understanding. It's also beneficial to take care of oneself by engaging in activities that make you feel good, including enjoying time with loved ones or pursuing a passion.

REPARENTING YOUR INNER CHILD

Giving yourself the attention, love, and support you might have been deprived of as a child is part of reparenting your inner child. You can see yourself speaking to your inner child as a kind and encouraging father, encouraging it with words of love and acceptance, and confirming its feelings and emotions.

The best course of action, if you're having trouble healing your inner child, is to seek expert assistance. Your childhood traumas can be addressed by a therapist or counselor, who can also offer you a secure and encouraging environment in which to express your feelings.

Keep in mind that it takes time and patience to reclaim your inner child. You can have a better relationship with yourself and let go of the unpleasant memories from your past by recognizing your inner child. You can recover and develop.

DEAR READER

I want to take a moment to offer my sincere gratitude as you turn the last pages of this book. I appreciate you taking the time to read my words, allowing me to share my thoughts and ideas with you, and joining me on this journey.

It has been an amazing adventure, full of ups and downs, times of clarity, and periods of doubt, to write this book. One thing, though, has been constant throughout it all: my gratitude to you, the reader.

You are the one who brought meaning into these pages, made the journey worthwhile, and gave this book purpose. Your openness, curiosity, and eagerness to discuss these concepts have brought this book to life in ways I never could have predicted.

As you finish this book, I hope you experience the inspiration and a sense of accomplishment. The most important thing to me is that you leave these pages with fresh eyes, new understandings, and fresh concepts to guide you through the rest of the world.

Again, I want to thank you for joining me on this

adventure. Then I can say, I appreciate your support and being here. I wish you all the best till we cross each other's paths again in the future.

Sincerely,

Nikki Sheikh

nikkisheikh.com

coachnikkisheikh@gmail.com

ACKNOWLEDGMENTS

Although writing a book is a solitary activity, it is not a solo accomplishment. A book needs a village to make it, and I am appreciative of everyone who has contributed to mine.

I want to start by expressing my gratitude to my family for their continuous support and inspiration. I am appreciative of their affection and tolerance for giving me the time, space, and resources I required to write this book.

I owe a debt of gratitude to my friends and coworkers who supported me along the journey by providing comments, inspiration, and encouragement. I appreciate your thoughtfulness, compassion, and willingness to read through my draughts since it made all the difference.

Finally, I want to thank my readers, who have given me the greatest gift of all: the opportunity to share my words with the world. Your interest, support, and feedback have made this journey all the more rewarding, and I am humbled and grateful to be able to call myself a writer.

Thank you all for being a part of this journey with me.

ABOUT THE AUTHOR

Nikki Sheikh is a well-known author and influencer who has a passion for helping others in realizing their full potential and live their best lives. She was raised in a middle-class household in a small town in Maharashtra. Nikki started her career as a software engineer after receiving a degree in computer science, working for top tech firms.

She developed an interest in human psychology and the law of attraction and delved deeply into the field of personal growth. To learn more about the mind and how people may use their inner strength to create the life they want, Nikki read books, went to seminars, and took courses.

As Nikki's interest in personal growth expanded, she started writing to share her knowledge. She wrote several books, including "Raise Your Vibration: Live A Happy And Grateful Life," which has assisted countless individuals all over the world in making positive changes in their life.

A popular speaker and coach, Nikki is renowned for her uplifting and encouraging message. She uses her knowledge of human psychology and personal development to empower people to take charge of their life and design the future they want. Nikki's goal is to motivate and encourage others to reach their full potential and live their best life.

9 798890 262301

Printed by Libri Plureos GmbH in Hamburg,
Germany